Excel
Tips and Tricks

M.L. HUMPHREY

SELECT TITLES BY M.L. HUMPHREY

EXCEL ESSENTIALS
Excel for Beginners
Intermediate Excel
50 Useful Excel Functions
50 More Excel Functions

EXCEL 365 ESSENTIALS
Excel 365 for Beginners
Intermediate Excel 365
102 Useful Excel 365 Functions

EXCEL ESSENTIALS 2019
Excel 2019 Beginner
Excel 2019 Intermediate
Excel 2019 Formulas & Functions

See mlhumphrey.com for Microsoft Word, PowerPoint and Access titles and more

CONTENTS

Introduction

This book is a short collection of all the little tips and tricks I've found over the years that help me work faster in Microsoft Excel. Most of them come from my Excel beginner books. (Each of my Excel series are divided into beginner, intermediate, and formulas & functions titles.)

I'm going to assume here that you're already familiar with the basics of Excel like opening a file and navigating within Excel. (If not, check out one of those books).

Also, the descriptions in this book are shorter than the descriptions in the main series. This is just a quick and easy discussion of a few little tips and tricks, not us sitting down for an in-depth discussion.

If you like what you read, the conclusion tells you where you can go from here if you want to learn more from me. As I've said before and will say again, there are plenty of Excel resources out there. What I do is serve as a guide so you don't get bogged down in all the many, many, many things that Excel can do that you probably don't need.

Okay, so with that said, let's just dive right in.

Terminology

In case any of the terms I use in this book are unfamiliar to you or used in a way that is unique to me, here is a brief run-down of terms you might see in this book. (A full discussion of each term is covered in the beginner books, this is just a brief mention.)

Workbook

A workbook is what Excel likes to call an Excel file.

Worksheet

Excel defines a worksheet as the primary document you use in Excel to store and work with your data. A worksheet is organized into Columns and Rows that form Cells. A workbook can contain multiple worksheets.

Columns

Excel uses columns and rows to display information. Columns run across the top of the worksheet and, unless you've done something funky with your settings, are identified using letters of the alphabet.

Rows

Rows run down the side of each worksheet and are numbered starting at 1 and up to a very high number.

Column and row numbers are locational information. The first row will always be numbered 1, the first column will always be Column A. There will also always be a fixed number of rows and columns in each worksheet regardless of how many rows or columns of data you delete, add, or move around.

Cells

Cells are where the row and column data comes together. Cells are identified using the letter for the column and the number for the row that intersect to form that cell. For example, Cell A1 is the cell that is in the first column and first row of the worksheet.

Click

If I tell you to click on something, that means to move the cursor to a specific location and left-click or right-click on the option. If you left-click, this selects the item. If you right-click, this generally displays a dropdown list of options to choose from. If I don't tell you which to do, left- or right-click, then left-click.

Data

Data is the information you enter into your worksheet.

Data Table

I may also sometimes refer to a data table or table of data. This is just a combination of cells that contain related data in them.

Tab

Tabs are the options you have to choose from at the top of the workspace. The default tab names are File, Home, Insert, Page Layout, Formulas, Data, Review, View, and Help. But there are certain times when additional tabs will appear, for example, when you create a pivot table or a chart.

(This should not be confused with the Tab key which can be used to move across cells.)

Dropdown Menus

A dropdown menu is a listing of available choices that you can see when you right-click in certain places such as the main workspace or on a worksheet name. You will also see them when you click on an arrow next to or below an option in the top menu.

Dialogue Boxes

Dialogue boxes are pop-up boxes that contain additional choices.

Task Pane

On occasion Excel will open a task pane, which is different from a dialogue box because it is part of the workspace. These will normally appear on the right-hand side in Excel for certain tasks such as working with pivot tables or charts or using the built-in Help function.

Scroll Bars

When you have more information than will show in a screen, dialogue box, or dropdown menu, you will see scroll bars on the right side or bottom that allow you to navigate to see the rest of the information.

Formula Bar

The formula bar is the long white bar at the top of the main workspace directly below the top menu options that lets you see the actual contents of a cell, not just the display value.

Cell Notation

Cells are referred to by their column and row position. So Cell A1 is the cell that's the intersection of the first column and first row in the worksheet.

When written in Excel you just use A1, you do not need to include the word cell. A colon (:) can be used to reference a range of cells. A comma (,) can be used to separate cell references.

When in doubt about how to define a cell range, click into a cell, type =, and then go and select the cells you want to reference. Excel will describe your selection in the formula bar using cell notation.

Paste Special Values

Paste Special Values is a way of pasting copied values that keeps the calculation results or the cell values but removes any formulas or formatting.

Shortcuts

One of the key things you should learn when working in Excel are keyboard shortcuts. In the tables below, the header row tells you which key(s) to hold down (Ctrl, Ctrl + Shift, etc.). The Task column tells you what that key will do when paired with each letter.

For example, if you hold down the Ctrl and n key at the same time (Ctrl + N), that will open a new file.

Ctrl +	Task
N	New File
O	Open File
S	Save File
C	Copy
V	Paste
X	Cut
Z	Undo
F	Open Find and Replace Dialogue Box to Find tab
A	Select All
P	Print
W	Close Current Workbook
B	Bold/Unbold Selected Text
I	Italicize/Remove Italics From Selected Text
U	Underline/Remove Underline From Selected Text
1	Open Format Cells Dialogue Box

Ctrl +	Task
End	Go to Last Column of Blank Worksheet OR Go to Last Column In Data Range OR Go to Next Column to the Right With Data
Home	Go to First Column of Blank Worksheet OR Go to First Column in Data Range OR Go to Next Column to the Left with Data
Down Arrow	Go to Last Row of Blank Worksheet OR Go to Last Row In Data Range OR Go to Next Row Down That Contains Data
Up Arrow	Go to First Row of Blank Worksheet OR Go to First Row In Data Range OR Go to Next Row Up That Contains Data
Right Arrow	Go to Last Column of Blank Worksheet OR Go to Last Column In Data Range OR Go to Next Column to the Right With Data
Left Arrow	Go to First Column of Blank Worksheet OR Go to First Column in Data Range OR Go to Next Column to the Left with Data

Note above that both the End and Home keys and Right and Left arrows have the same behavior listed. You may need to experiment on your computer to see which one works this way for you. On my laptop the Home and End keys are combined with the Left and Right arrow keys so it's basically just the arrow keys that do this. This may apply for the Ctrl + Shift shortcuts that involve right arrows as well.

Alt +	Task
S	Refresh Pivot Table
H	Access Menu Options, Use Alt + Letter(s)/Number(s) to Select Task to Perform
Tab	Move Between Open Programs in Windows

Ctrl + Shift	Task
$	Format as Currency
#	Format as Date
!	Format as Number with Comma For Thousands
%	Format as Percent
Right Arrow	Select All Cells in Range To Right
Down Arrow	Select All Cells In Range Downward
Right and then Down Arrow	Select All Cells in Range Across and Down

Other	Task
Esc	Exit a Cell, Back Out of a Function, Close a Tool, General Escape Option
Tab	Move to the Right One Cell
Shift + Tab	Move to the Left One Cell
Windows Key + Ctrl + O	Open On-Screen Keyboard

Navigation

I discuss in detail how to navigate Excel in the beginner guides, but here are just a few tips and tricks.

Pin a File

If you ever have a file that you always want readily accessible but that won't stay in your recent files listing because you open enough files that it sometimes falls out of your top ten most recent, then you can Pin that file and it will always be available to you in your Pinned files section.

To do this, find the file in your recent files list on the File Open screen. Hold your cursor over that listing. You should see the image of a thumbtack appear on the right-hand side. If you hold your cursor over that image it will say, "Pin this item to the list".

Click on that thumbtack. If you then click onto the Pinned option, that file will be listed there. And it will stay there regardless of what other files you open, so that it's always available to you.

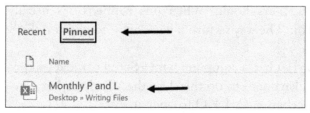

Once you've pinned a file, you can open it by going to your Pinned Files section and clicking on that name.

Navigate Between Worksheets

There are a number of ways to move between worksheets in Excel, but one trick when you have more worksheets than you can see in your workspace is to right-click on one of the arrows at the left-end of the worksheet listing. This will bring up an Activate dialogue box that lists all of your worksheets:

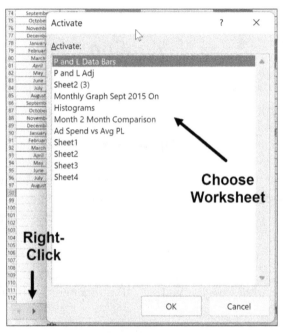

From there click on the name of the worksheet you want and then click on OK and Excel will take you to that worksheet.

Turn Off Scroll Lock

On occasion I will find that navigating in Excel isn't working the way I'm used to. I arrow and things don't move like they should. When this happens, it's usually because Scroll Lock somehow was turned on. The way to turn it back off is to click on the Scroll Lock key on your keyboard.

Unfortunately, I haven't had a computer with a Scroll Lock key in probably a decade, so you have to open a virtual keyboard to do this. Use the Windows key (the one with four squares to the left of your spacebar) + Ctrl + O to open it.

(Another option is to go through your Start menu to Settings and search for keyboard there and then toggle the on-screen keyboard to on.)

The keyboard will appear on your screen and look something like this:

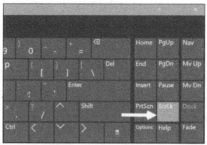

The Scroll Lock key (ScrLk) should be colored when it's turned on. It's one of the right-hand side options on the keyboard. Click on it to turn it off and close the virtual keyboard. Excel will return to acting normally.

Freeze Panes

Freeze Panes lets you keep certain information, such as a header row, visible in your workspace while you scroll down to see more data. Without freeze panes you end up with a screen full of data but nothing that tells you what that data is.

If all you want is to freeze the top row of your worksheet or the first column, go to the Window section of the View tab and click on the dropdown arrow for Freeze Panes.

Choose either Freeze Top Row or Freeze First Column.

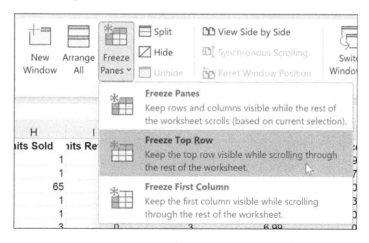

You can do one or the other this way, but not both. If you want to freeze more than one column, more than one row, or columns and rows both at the same time, then you need to first click into your worksheet at the first cell that you are okay *not* seeing.

In other words, below the rows that you want to freeze in place and to the right of the columns that you want to freeze in place.

Once you've done that, go to the Freeze Panes dropdown and choose the first option, Freeze Panes, to keep your desired rows and columns visible.

To remove freeze panes, just go back to that same dropdown menu. The top option will now be Unfreeze Panes.

Input & Formatting

F2

If you click on a cell and use F2, your cursor will appear at the end of the text in that cell and you can then quickly edit the contents of the cell without having to go to the formula bar. Note that not all computers have F2 as the default option these days so you may need to change that setting or use the Fn key to access it.

Display Cell Contents as Text

If you have an entry like January 2020 or =A1+B1 that you want to have display in a cell as text, place a single quotation mark at the start of the text.

'January 2020

'=A1+B1

The single quote mark will not be visible in the cell, only in the formula bar. But it will keep Excel from converting that entry into a date or treating it like a formula.

Include Line Breaks In a Cell

Another thing you might find yourself wanting to do is to include text in a cell, but have it break across lines. So, for example, you may want an entry that looks like this:

where the A, the B, and the C are all on separate lines.

You can't just use Enter because that will take you to the next cell. What you have to do is use Alt + Enter. So hold down the Alt key as you hit Enter and that will create a line break within the cell.

Convert Number Stored as Text

Excel will flag cells with "errors" using a green triangle in the top left corner. Click on a flagged cell and an error triangle will appear. Hold your mouse over that triangle and you'll see a dropdown arrow. Click on that to see the dropdown menu:

The first line in the dropdown tells you that the error in this cell is that the number is stored as text. You can fix that by clicking on Convert To Number just below that.

To convert all cells in a column at once, select all of the cells first. You should see the warning triangle next to the top cell in the range. Click on the dropdown arrow and select the convert option. That will convert all of the selected cells, not just the top one.

Merge & Center

Merge and Center is a specialized command that can come in handy when you're working with a table where you want a header that spans multiple columns of data.

What it does is merges the cells you select and then centers your text across those merged cells.

To use this option, first select all of the cells you want to merge. Next, go to the Alignment section of the Home tab and choose Merge & Center. This will combine your selected cells into one cell and center the contents from that left-uppermost cell across the selection.

Like so:

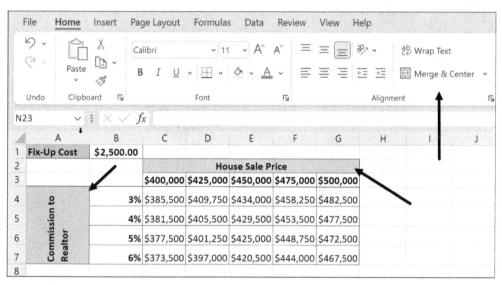

In the screenshot above I've merged and centered the text "House Sale Price" across Columns C through G in Row 2. I've also merged and centered the text "Commission to Realtor" across Rows 4 through 7 in Column A. (Note that I also changed the alignment of that text.)

If you ever need to unmerge merged cells you can do so by selecting the Unmerge Cells option from that dropdown.

You can also merge or unmerge cells by using the Merge Cells checkbox in the Alignment tab of the Format Cells dialogue box.

Merge & Center is also an option in the mini formatting menu. It's located in the top right corner of the menu. Clicking on it for previously merged cells will unmerge those cells.

(Don't merge cells if you plan to do a lot of data analysis with what you've input into the worksheet because it will mess with your ability to filter, sort, or use pivot tables. It's really for creating a finalized, pretty-looking report.)

Double-Click To Copy

If you want to copy down a formula or other value, you can often select the cell(s) you want to copy and then double-left click in the bottom right corner of the right-most cell of the selected range and Excel will copy those values down for you. This requires that the column(s) you're doing this with be adjacent to a larger data table so Excel knows how far down to copy the entries.

Sometimes Excel tries to turn the entries you're copying into a series, so changes the values, like it did here:

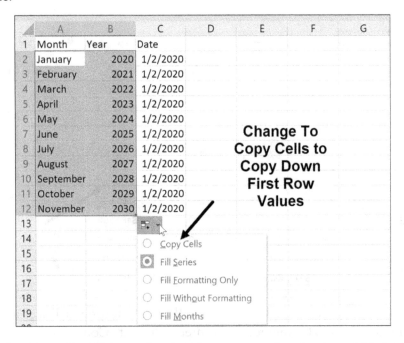

But you can fix this easily. Click on the dropdown arrow for the Auto Fill Options box that shows at the bottom right side of the series (shown in the image above) and change the option from Fill Series to Copy Cells.

Calculations

Calculations Without Formulas

If you just want to see a count, sum, or average of a range of values, the easiest way to do so is to select the cells and then look in the bottom right corner of your workspace where Excel by default will show those calculations.

You can right-click next to those calculations to bring up a dropdown menu where you can also choose to display numerical count, minimum, and maximum.

AutoSum

If you have a continuous range of data, Excel can build your SUM formula for you. Select the range and then click on the AutoSum option in the Editing section of the Home tab or in the Function Library section of the Formulas tab.

The AutoSum option has a dropdown menu that will also let you use Excel to calculate Average, Count Numbers, Max, and Min as well.

Be sure to review the formula it writes, because it will stop at a blank cell and sometimes can be confused as to whether you want to sum across a row or up a column.

Two-Variable Analysis Grid

A two-variable analysis grid allows you to quickly look at the possible outcomes for different combinations of two variables. For example, hours worked and hourly pay:

	A	B	C	D	E	F	G	H
1								
2						Hourly Pay		
3				15	16	17	18	19
4			20	$300	$320	$340	$360	$380
5		Hours Worked	25	$375	$400	$425	$450	$475
6			30	$450	$480	$510	$540	$570
7			35	$525	$560	$595	$630	$665
8			40	$600	$640	$680	$720	$760
9								
10		*Formula in Cell D4:*		=$C4*D$3				
11								

If you use $ signs to fix the cell references, you can build this table and only have to write one formula. Excel will adjust the formula for you when you copy it to all of the other cells.

The formula in Cell D4 here is:

=$C4*D$3

The $ sign in front of the C but not the 4 in C4 and in front of the 3 but not the D in D3 is what makes that work that way.

Printing

Print Top Row or Left Column on Each Printed Page

In Excel this is the Print Titles option. It can be found on the Sheet tab of the Page Setup dialogue box which you can access by clicking on Print Titles in the Page Setup section of the Page Layout tab:

Click into the field for "Rows to repeat at top" to select the row number(s) in your worksheet that you want to have repeat at the top of each page.

Click into the field for "Columns to repeat at left" to select the column(s) you want to repeat on each page.

You can repeat more than one row or column on each page, but if you do that, be careful that you don't end up selecting so many rows or columns to repeat that you basically just print the same thing over and over and over again. (Think of this as the printer equivalent of freeze panes if that helps.)

Custom Scaling

If you have a document you're trying to print and it overflows by just a little bit onto the next page, you can adjust that using the custom scaling setting. Excel will shrink the printed area to make it fit to your specified number of pages long and wide.

The custom scaling option is located on the Page tab of the Page Setup dialogue box.

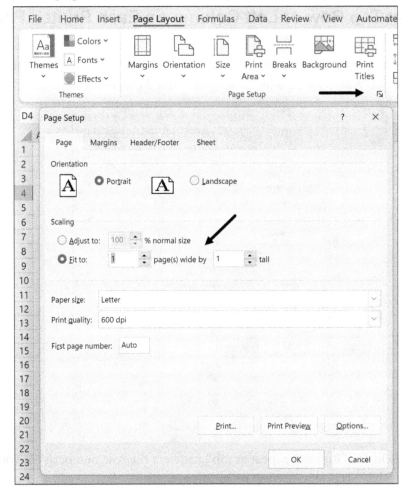

It can be opened by clicking on the arrow in the bottom right corner of the Page Setup section of the Page Layout tab.

In the scaling section, click on the option for Fit To and then choose how many pages wide and how many pages tall you want your document to be.

Excel will do whatever you tell it to, so be careful you don't make your text so small it can't be read.

Also, on the Print screen there are basic scaling options for Fit Sheet on One Page, Fit All Columns on One Page, and Fit All Rows on One Page under the No Scaling dropdown at the bottom of the options list. (I just find I usually need something like two pages by three.)

You can get to the custom option from that dropdown, too, by clicking on Custom Scaling Options at the bottom.

Conclusion

Okay. That was just a short set of quick tips and tricks that I use to make Excel easier and faster to work with, some of which I wish I'd known during my corporate career but have picked up while writing these books.

It is by no means a thorough introduction to any of the topics covered here. The Excel Essentials books when put together are an inch thick, so there is far, far more to Excel than this.

If you liked my way of explaining things and you want to learn more about Excel, then you may want to check one of those other books out.

The beginner titles, which most of this came from, are *Excel for Beginners, Excel 2019 Beginner*, and *Excel 365 for Beginners*. Each of those titles is designed to take you from absolute beginner through to about 95% of what you need to know to use Excel on a daily basis.

The intermediate titles, *Intermediate Excel, Excel 2019 Intermediate,* and *Intermediate Excel 365* explore more advanced topics like conditional formatting, pivot tables, and charts. So more focus on data analysis.

And then the final titles are the formulas and functions titles. The original series had two of them, *50 Useful Excel Functions* and *50 More Excel Functions*. The later series have just one, *Excel 2019 Formulas & Functions* and *102 Useful Excel 365 Functions*.

Which series is best for you will depend on which version of Excel you're using and who else you may need to work with.

If it's just you and you have Excel 2021 or Excel 365, then use the Excel 365 titles.

If you have Excel 2019 and aren't worried about working with anyone with an older version of Excel, then use the Excel 2019 books.

If you have an older version of Excel than 2019 or are working with people who have older versions of Excel, then the original Excel Essentials series is the one you want. That series was written to work for anyone in any version of Excel. It doesn't have the latest bells and whistles (like IFS or TEXTJOIN or XLOOKUP), but it also ensures that you can work with anyone in any version of Excel.

Okay. Hope this helped and you learned something you didn't know before. And hope maybe it prompted you to check out one of the other books, too.

Index

About the Author

M.L. Humphrey is a former stockbroker with a degree in Economics from Stanford and an MBA from Wharton who has spent close to twenty years as a regulator and consultant in the financial services industry.

You can reach M.L. at mlhumphreywriter@gmail.com or at mlhumphrey.com.

www.ingramcontent.com/pod-product-compliance
Lightning Source LLC
Chambersburg PA
CBHW060512060326
40689CB00020B/4721